YOUR KNOWLEDGE HAS VALUE

- We will publish your bachelor's and master's thesis, essays and papers

- Your own eBook and book - sold worldwide in all relevant shops

- Earn money with each sale

Upload your text at www.GRIN.com
and publish for free

Bibliographic information published by the German National Library:

The German National Library lists this publication in the National Bibliography; detailed bibliographic data are available on the Internet at http://dnb.dnb.de .

This book is copyright material and must not be copied, reproduced, transferred, distributed, leased, licensed or publicly performed or used in any way except as specifically permitted in writing by the publishers, as allowed under the terms and conditions under which it was purchased or as strictly permitted by applicable copyright law. Any unauthorized distribution or use of this text may be a direct infringement of the author s and publisher s rights and those responsible may be liable in law accordingly.

Imprint:

Copyright © 2018 GRIN Verlag
Print and binding: Books on Demand GmbH, Norderstedt Germany
ISBN: 9783668748576

This book at GRIN:

https://www.grin.com/document/432452

Tom Tanner

Policy brief on possible reforms of the UN-Security Council

GRIN Verlag

GRIN - Your knowledge has value

Since its foundation in 1998, GRIN has specialized in publishing academic texts by students, college teachers and other academics as e-book and printed book. The website www.grin.com is an ideal platform for presenting term papers, final papers, scientific essays, dissertations and specialist books.

Visit us on the internet:

http://www.grin.com/

http://www.facebook.com/grincom

http://www.twitter.com/grin_com

Policy brief on possible reforms of the UN-Security Council

Abstract

The United Nations Security council is a system with some deep implemented problems. Most important are the unproportionate representation of the United Nation's members and the inequality of voting power of its permanent members. It is of every, but those five permanent members interest that these flaws are fixed. This paper elaborates three different approaches to do so for Austria. First, the removal of the permanent member status or at least its right to veto resolutions. Second, the withdrawal from the United Nations while forming a new supranational organisation. And last, the option to bide for a better opportunity to implement one of the other policies and to avoid negative consequences. There are positive as well as negative consequences to each of those policies which are discussed separately. Secluding this policy brief will come to the conclusion that the formal proposal is the best option for Austria at the moment.

Keywords: UNO, UNSC, reform, Austria

Word count: 2 155

Table of Content

1. Introduction	3
2. Statement of Issue	3
3. Options	5
3. A. Abolition of the P5	5
3. B. Withdrawal from the UNO	5
3. C. Bide	7
4. Summary	7
5. Bibliography	9

1. Introduction

The United Nations Organization (UNO) often also just United Nations (UN) where finally formed in 1945 after efforts going back up to 1939. Thus, it is the spiritual successor of the League of Nations which failed for numerous reasons. Among them where for example that the major world powers where never at the same time member of the League, no general prohibition of war and the selfish blockade of resolutions respectively voting behaviour from powerful and influential members. Although the first two of those where solved by forming a new intergovernmental Organization, the UN, especially the last of those issues is one that is still challenging today and calls for reform have been frequent.

The five permanent members of the Security Council (P5) have in contrary to the other ten temporary members a right to veto every resolution, therefore in proportionate power in comparison to everyone else. In addition, the representation inside the council regarding the permanent members is very western NATO preferring.

Hence it is every nation's concern to get reforms on the UN initiated, the following chapter is going to go deeper into the UNSC's problems. Chapter three is going to explain tree different options on how Austria's position in the upcoming UN-general assembly (UNGA) could look like. In chapter four will be a short summary of the issues with the United Nations Security Council (UNSC) and finally the policy recommendation to bring in a formal proposal at the United Nations General Assembly to abolish the permanent membership and/or the right to veto.

2. Statement of issue

There are two[1] big issues with how the United Nations Security Council works since it was formed in 1945. First, the *veto power*: The most important and strongest victorious powers of WW II, who are more or less coincidently also the only states who legally own and operate[2] nuclear weapons according to Treaty on the Non-Proliferation of Nuclear Weapons, France, the United stated of America, the United Kingdom, the Soviet Union[3] and the republic of

---

[1] Often explained as more, but condensed here
[2] Excluding nuclear participation of Belgium, Germany, Italy, the Netherlands, and Turkey here
[3] Respectively the Russian Federation

China[4] are fitted with an unconditional veto. Meaning, any of those permanent Council members can basically infringe any international law they please without any institutional consequences whatsoever. Although when asked, it is often but weakly argued that like this, the major global powers are forced to come to compromise or even consent on global conflict issues, but history as well as presence prove that statement wrong. The only peacebuilding achievement, and one has to leave that to them, is the successful prevention of open wars between those major powers. Thus, it could be argued that the United Nations Security Council is in fact an oligarchical system, keeping everyone on the outside of the permanent council loge down. This circumstance alone displays already that the Security council System was rigged right from the drawing board and the only effect of the Veto power is a cartel-like instrument to keep as much power in relation to non P5 states as possible. Accepting this fact, one must also accept that the attempt to increase the number of permanent members like in the Annan plan (A) in 2005 (Mingst & Karns, 2012, 51) is not only not going to happen, considering the fact that for a step like that would require that none of the existing P5 would veto it, but that it would hinder the purposes[5] of the United Nations Charter (UN Charter, art. 1). In other words, more Nations with veto right would render the situation even worse by making resolutions harder to achieve.

Second, the *disproportional representation* of the members within the security council: There is a massive misrepresentation regarding the members of the united Nations within the security council. Not only does the right to veto of the P5 violate the UN Charter[6] itself, it also gives unfair advantage to regions. For example, there is no African or south American[7] state permanent member, but three European[8] ones. In addition, and maybe the most dangerous issue with the functional principle of the security council, it overrepresents North Atlantic Treaty Organization members having three out of five NATO members in the P5. Taking for example the war in Syria that is taking place at this moment, the international law braking NATO bombardments since the 15th of September 2014[9] (Ganser, 2017, 315-318)

---

[4]Respectively the People's Republic of China
[5]International peace and security, friendly relations between nations, co-operation in solving international problems of an economic, social, cultural, or humanitarian character and to be a centre for harmonizing the actions of nations
[6] "The Organization is based on the principle of the sovereign equality of all its Members." (UN Charter, art. 2 (1))
[7] Not counting France as south American
[8] Counting the Russian Federation as European
[9] Starting with United States of America, the United Kingdom, Turkey and France [in that order]

show the catastrophic potential the mechanics of the United Nations Security Council has. Not only, as mentioned above, can the P5 invade any country they please without having to fear any institutional consequences, but assuming just one Syrian bomber would be able and willing to penetrate Turkish airspace and carry out a counterstrike, comprises the risk that the North Atlantic Treaty Organization member Turkey pleads towards the alliance case as in The North Atlantic Treaty Art. 5, dragging the remaining North Atlantic Treaty Organization states into a case for the alliance. Although illegitimate, this is exactly what the French minister of defence Jean-Yves Le Drian tried to argue towards the European Union, following the terrorist attacks in Paris in November 2015. Registering these problems, one has to admit that the United Nations and even more so the United Nations Security Council, is in fact in the middle of a global security dilemma.

3. Options

3. A. Abolition of the permanent 5

Austria could bring in a formal proposal at the United Nations General Assembly to abolish the right to veto and/or the permanent membership at the United Nations Security Council. This option would have most likely purely symbolic character since 9/15 UNSC members would have to vote in favor of such a reform, plus none of the P5 would have to veto it, which as mentioned earlier, is very unlikely. In contrast to this claim, is the United Nations General Assembly Resolution 377 that was adopted in 1950 to lever out the Soviet veto regarding the deployment of UN-troops in the Korean War. This incident shows the institutional power of the United Nations Security Council is not irrevocably. That same so called "Uniting for Peace" resolution states that "[…] because of a lack of unanimity amongst its five permanent members, fails to act as required to maintain international peace and security, the General Assembly shall consider the matter immediately and may issue any recommendations it deems necessary in order to restore international peace and security." (UN res. 377, 1950). It could be argued that the history of conflicts since the formation of the United Nations Security Council is proof of its inability to act as required to maintain international peace and security.

3. B. Withdrawal from the United Nations Organization

Since there is no point in being part of a flawed and unfair system, we could drop out from the United Nations Organization. Since the idea of an intergovernmental Organization with the goals to ensure world peace, and to aid with international problems is very noble and sensible, we could form a new intergovernmental Organization and in the same breath invite all countries to join in. This organisation could even work very similar to the existing United Nations, but without any permanent members in the Security Council or even without one altogether. Decisions on security issues could also be made in a general assembly restoring the sovereign equality of all its members. Those decisions may become legally binding and require a two-thirds majority. As a result, the organization might become less effective, but in the same breath way fairer. Considering the Vienna Convention on the law of treaties from 1969, this option would be hard to legitimize legally. Bearing in mind that it introduced the principle of *rebus sic stantibus*, meaning that a state may only withdraw from treaty without a provision for the withdrawal, which the UN charter is, if "A fundamental change of circumstances which has occurred with regard to those existing at the time of the conclusion of a treaty, and which was not foreseen by the parties, may not be invoked as a ground for terminating or withdrawing from the treaty [...]" (Vienna Convention on the law of treaties, art. 61 & 62).

Since the inner logic of the existing United Nations Organization forbids such fundamental changes this step would be not a legal one. Additionally, and most likely also one without direct legal consequences. Indirect there would be numerous consequences like a stop of cooperation with the different branches of the united nations and loan from the World bank. Considering the relative wealth and peaceful environment the Austrian republic finds itself in, these consequences would be less of a problem for us than for other nations to join a new international society, discouraging them to follow us. Beholding the fact that forming a new version of the United Nations is a major threat to the power of the permanent five, we should brace ourselves for some kind of attempted regime change. This could include but is not limited to: assassination attempts on high ranking government members, legitimisation of sanctions, legitimization of an invasion and causing turmoil within the constitutive people. It is well known that the permanent United Nations Security Council members carry out similar operations in countries who do not act as they please like in Cuba 1961, Iraq 2003 or Libya 2011 on a regular basis (Ganser, 2017, 335–337). The only United Nations withdrawal in history was in 1956 by Indonesia as a result of Malaysia gaining a temporary seat in the security council. After 18 months, losing 50 million US dollars aid from the UN Educational, Scientific and Cultural Organization and the World Health Organization (Webster, 2011, 253) and a military coup supported by the United States Central Intelligence Agency (Weiner, 2007, 143-153), Indonesia returned to the United Nations without any obstacles.

3. C. Bide

We could do nothing and go along with the status quo. This way we would avoid any of the negative consequences mentioned in Option A and B. This is especially important with regard to the Austrian involvement of the death of nine Syrian secret police members in the UN-buffer zone at the Israeli-Syrian border in 2012. Depending on the outcome of the investigations, and maybe even more important, how our international public image will be perceived as a consequence, this case could be used to argue against Austria and that we try to avoid consequences that way. Additionally, they could argue that we are international lawbreakers ourselves. Either way we could live down the Golan-case and wait for a better time to implement one of the other options. On the negative side this policy changes nothing and the Issues with the United Nations Security Council remain.

4. Summary

There are several issues with the UNSC, but in this paper they are condensed into the two most important ones.

1. The right to Veto of the P5
2. The disproportional representation within the P5

I have elaborated tree possible options on how to cope with those problems. None of them include increasing the number of permanent Security Council members, like previous reform efforts proposed on purpose, because I think it would only worsen the situation. The elaborated options are

> A. A formal and most likely purely symbolic proposal at the UNGA to eliminate the permanent membership at the UNSC

B. A complete withdrawal from the UNO and forming a new intergovernmental organization
C. Doing nothing

Policy recommendation: Considering the possible negative effects of option B and the lack of effects of option C, I recommend *option A*, the *formal proposal to eliminate the permanent membership* in the UNSC. This way other nations have the chance to join in while denoting the general atmosphere towards the P5 without taking too radical steps immediately. If and when enough nations agree on our proposal there is still time to conduct option B.

5. Bibliography

Ganser, Daniele. *Illegale Kriege: Wie die NATO- Länder die UNO sabotieren.* Zürich: Orell Füssli, 2017.

Mingst, Karen A., and Karns, Margaret P. *The United Nations in the 21st Century: Dilemmas in World Politics.* Boulder: Westview Press, 2012.

North Atlantic Treaty. Available at https://www.nato.int/cps/ic/natohq/official_texts_17120.htm last visit 13.05.18.

UN Charta. Available at http://www.un.org/en/sections/un-charter/chapter-i/index.html. Last visit. 12.05.18.

UNGA Resolution 377. Available at http://www.un.org/en/sc/repertoire/otherdocs/GAres377A(v).pdf. Last visit 13.05.18.

Vienna Convention on the law of treaties. Available at https://treaties.un.org/doc/publication/unts/volume%201155/volume-1155-i-18232-english.pdf. Last visit 12.05.18.

Webster, David. 2011. "Development advisors in a time of cold war and decolonization: The United Nations Technical Assistance Administration, 1950–59" *Journal of Global History* 6, no. 2 (2011): 249–272.

Weiner, Tim. "Legacy of Ashes: The History of the CIA" *Journal of Urban Research* 3, (2007): 143-153.

YOUR KNOWLEDGE HAS VALUE

- We will publish your bachelor's and master's thesis, essays and papers

- Your own eBook and book - sold worldwide in all relevant shops

- Earn money with each sale

Upload your text at www.GRIN.com and publish for free